Whisp

of a

Loud Soul

Whispers

of a

Loud Soul

Mya G. Wolf

Whispers of a Loud Soul

ISBN: 979-8-7448-3130-1

Contents

For my Aunt Audrey

My guardian angel and butterfly

Thank you for always looking over me

I love you

I.

Questioning

I heard the voice for the first time amidst the
chaos of my mind

Whispers of a Loud Soul buried deep inside

She felt familiar

I had known her before

She was sacred and came from my core

This is the story of Her

The Loud Soul that speaks so gently

This is also the story of Me

Of how I questioned everything

I found Her when I was searching for Myself

The voice that longs to speak to us all

And if we listen

We can find Her

Longing Outside of Myself

I would find myself gazing out my window

Late at night unable to sleep

Wondering if I would ever find peace

I questioned everything

Not knowing why

I hoped I would find my answers in the sky

Written clearly in the stars

A message just for me

Please tell me who I am

Where I am going

And who I will be

Younger Self

She walked the halls of her high school feeling misplaced

Like a rainbow trying to show off her colors during a storm

While others were solving equations

She wondered what it would feel like to fly

Though she kept her wings hidden

At night she felt closest to the moon

And discussed her dreams with the stars

The universe tugged softly at her heart

Whispering in her ear

Reminding her there was nothing to fear

The Cage I Made

I have locked myself in this cage

I press the key against my heart

I could be free

But my cage keeps me safe

I could fly

But my wings keep me warm

For this cage is so cold

Be Free

She began to listen to the little voice in her heart
that told her to run

Away from the pointless chatter

The toxic relationships

And never-ending social ladder

Because none of it really mattered

None of these things would set her free

Make Them Proud

I stare at myself and see the little girl and the woman in me staring back. The little girl can move mountains. She is fearless and creative. The woman is always one step ahead, moving with ease as I try to keep up. They both want me to light the fire that burns within me. Can I be what they want me to be?

Uncomfortable

There are parts of me I hate

And they will remain this way

Until I am brave enough to show them grace

Secretly I am just afraid

Of shining light on what brings me pain

It is easier to blame my demons

Than to ask from where they came

Darkness is only evil if you allow it to be

Loud Soul

How do I surrender

To a soul

So unpredictably free

Kind yet fierce

Gently untamed

Light and stone

Slow Down

Slow down

Even when it feels like you are running out of
time

Those heavy stones on your wings are temporary

And when they fall away

You will fly

Scars

One day

Your scars will become

The road

That leads you home

Questioning

Why are we so eager to get to tomorrow?

If everyone was as comfortable as they claim to be

Wouldn't we be able to settle into the present effortlessly?

Layers

We wear the clothes of our elders, our families
and friends

Holding onto pieces of "shoulds" and "woulds" as
if they are meant to be ours

Masks and heavy jewelry, nearly burdensome,
draping us in outdated beliefs

A collection of "Who do you want me to be?"
rather than "Who am I?"

We forget where we come from

It is time to stop playing the part

It is time to stop pretending to be who we are not

For we are children of the moon and stars

And our light begs to shine through the darkness
that is not ours

Endings

Will I survive if I let go of the things that were not even mine to begin with?

Drifting Away

My heart aches

Knowing it is time to move on

I am no longer

Who you want me to be

I think I am sorry

But a part of me

Is eager to see

What else has been waiting for me

Dark is Light

What is the point of life

If I cannot make love to every aspect of myself

Even the darkest parts of me crave love

Even the darkest parts of you long for
understanding

A Letter to Myself

I am sorry for letting you down all of this time.

12:34

Happiness shouldn't come with a catch

I Am Not Your Hero

It is not my job to bring out the greatness in you

Maybe one day you will let your light shine through

Our Dreams Dream of Us too

We complicate our dreams

To keep them far away

But really

They sit in one place

Waiting for the day

We decide we are worthy enough to move forward

Leaving old illusions behind

Endings pt. 2

Her chest rises and falls

Her heart sinks deep into her body

She sees stars within the chaos

Longing for a sense of peace

She cries with herself through the night

Gently releasing the thoughts

Weaving within her mind

On the Right Path

And even when lost at sea, those treacherous
waves are where you are meant to be.

40

Changing of the Seasons

When the seasons change

And you are forced to shed your skin

Remember that you will rise again

When your world shatters

And the illusions melt away

Remember that you will rise again

Just as the trees shed their leaves

And the caterpillar grows its wings

We will all rise again

April I

How can I be so happy and so sad at the same time?

How selfish of me to up and leave

But how bold of me to carry on...

Am I brave for putting myself first?

Left broken

Maybe cracked open

Waiting for some light to seep in

April II

She is so beautiful

The woman who kept going without you

I think I'd like to meet her

Ask of her regrets

She would only laugh

And I would realize that her song

Was the light I longed for all along

Thank you

Your lack of love reflected

The lack of love I gave myself

Thank you for revealing this hole in me

So I could fill it so graciously

II.

Surrender

Self-Love I

Staring at myself until the judgement fades

Loving myself as hard as I would love another

Telling myself that I am worthy

Crying my old beliefs away

Worthy

Give yourself grace when all is well

Give yourself grace when all is falling apart

You are worthy of feeling the light

Even when lost in the dark

Fraud

It's easy to show up as anything but yourself

Exhale

Honor your deaths and life becomes your masterpiece

Breathing Through Our Seasons

There is a divinity within our breath. We inhale life and exhale what is to be left behind. Our breath is our sacred rhythm. Our breath reminds us that our cycles and seasons bring balance.

Every day we live with the sun and fall asleep with the moon. And every day the sun rises, and we reawaken. Taking in another breath, we have the opportunity to climb out of bed and surrender to the divine seasons of the universe.

Creator

You create the magic

You are the dreamer, after all

Yes, the bigger you allow yourself to dream,

The bigger you could fall

But a life without magic

Is no life at all

Infinite

As soon as we accept the future as limitless

We can let go of the infinity of the past

Beauty of Being

To be human means

We get to observe beauty

And be beauty

At the same time

Realizations

Home comes from the comfort of the soul

Infinite

The more I love Myself

The more I love You

The more I love You

The more I love Myself

Vulnerability

It is okay to melt into the lap of another

To cry in a friend's arms until your eyes are empty

There is so much beauty in vulnerability

Opening yourself up like a flower is a gift to give

Your tears water the Earth

And the smile that comes after will fill their souls

Miracles

You were so unexpected

A true surprise

Innocent and sweet

Am I worthy of you?

Do I deserve your kindness?

If I let your love in

Will I lose you?

Or can I safely surrender

And welcome you with open arms?

Do I love myself enough

To let you in?

A Letter to You

Your love gives me faith

In all of the dreams

Passing through my fragile heart

That you hold so gently

Thank you

Imposter Syndrome

Take me to the top

But what if I'm not enough?

What if I fall?

What if I fail?

That is something I cannot handle

Or maybe

Every failure

Is taking me closer to the place I've always dreamed
of

A place where I am seen and heard

A place where I am strong

And I can change people's lives with my voice

My words

My song

Oh Baby

Just let go

You will be okay

Surrendering

I fall back into my body

Where it is safe to sing my song

Listening gently

My tired soul sings along

Whispers dancing through skin and bone

Healing my wounds

Bringing me home

5d

It seems as though nature is moving in slow motion

I notice the leaves falling

Each bird's cry a different tone

The sun feels warmer

The sky is brighter

I sense the portal between me and everything else

It feels familiar

Peaceful and welcoming

If I sit for long enough

I enter the place we all long for

Not given to me

Simply waiting for me to realize

That it has been there all along

Surrendering II

My body surrenders to the Earth

I fall to the ground

And let the sun melt my skin

Until all that is left

Is my being

I wait

The roots recharge me

The sky reflects back to me

A vision only my heart knows

A remembrance of my Loud Soul

Buried underneath my flesh and bone

Disguised as the wishes of others

Hidden by worry and regret

I let everything fall away

Transmuted by sacred land

Becoming who I truly am

Trust

Again, I crumble

Yet I have no fear

I know in time

I will get back up

A better person than before

I Am

Divine

I am Divine

It took me

All of this time

Finally

I remember

I am Divine

Calm After the Storm

And through the chaos we find ourselves

III.

Becoming

Short Story

When I finally crawled onto the path my heart
always longed to follow, the Earth stood still. The
trees held their breath, and the birds stopped
their song. Witnessing me discover the road that
had been beckoning me for so long. Praying I
would not run away out of fear. Praying I would
stay, despite my uncertainty. The sleeves of my
white dress fell below my shoulders, as I stooped
toward the ground. I did not notice. For the first
time in a while, I could feel the hum of the Earth
beneath my body. I felt natural, and I knew this
was where I was meant to be. This was an

initiation. A ceremony of the mind and body and spirit. Drums beat in the distance. Angels played their bells in excitement. The leaves began to glow, and the path set fire. I knew it was time to run. My feet kicked up dirt. I moved so fast; my white dress peeled away like snakeskin. My tears glimmered, signaling the forest that I had arrived. My long hair was now a mane. The tiger stripes on my hips deeply engraved, showing my strength. I howled with the wolves that ran alongside me. The wind whipped the trees, and thunder cheered me on.

Finally, I fell to my knees and let the grass take the rest of me. I was new. A single flower bloomed. There was no more path before me. My

direction was for me to decide. So, I closed my

eyes and let the whispers of my Loud Soul be my

guide.

Burn it Down

Do you dare to light the fire within you? The fire that will burn down everything you have ever known.

The fire that will show you the truth as your illusions melt away. Leaving you alone with your light.

Resistance

You can blow out the flame, but it will always come back.

Begging to help you rise.

You Didn't Kill Me

To all of the demons

That have made me feel unsafe

Less than and unworthy

Thank you

I am stronger than ever

Self-love II

I choose to see the beauty all around me. The glimmer of sunlight bouncing off my eyelashes as I observe the world before me.

The way the leaves on the trees wave hello on a windy day. Inviting me to explore the deepest parts of myself.

I know the beauty I see is also within me, for we are not separate beings. We are one universe, one song.

Self-love III

The freedom she felt

As she began to understand

That she could hold her own hand

She is her own biggest fan

Allowed to love herself more than any man

Her shame melted away

As this new partnership took form

One of the mind body and spirit

She was her own muse

And the idea of separation was no more

Becoming

And even though I lost what, in my mind, was
most important

I still survived.

Mama Tree

I bury my toes in the earth and grow roots into
the ground

I smile

For a woman with strong roots can never be
blown down

Inner Child

I forgot how it felt

To feel at peace

To feel pure joy

For so long I shut myself down

I felt so little

My world was black and white

And now I feel so much

Letting myself cry and laugh and sing

Every single day

Remembering what it was like

To be a child

Innocent and sweet

Healing those around me

Thank God I am me again

Thank God I set my mind aside

And instead set my soul on fire

Everything is colorful

Everyone is bright

Together we rise by recognizing our light

We Are One

When we go outside, we casually see,

The difference of every flower, bee, and tree

Trunk of an oak scarred by a storm

Mountains cracked and aged, delicately worn

We look into a mirror or scroll through our feed

Our differences turn into you vs. me

Immediately turned off if we are not perfectly thin

Divided by our weight and the color of our skin

Every tree a different size

Every flower a different color

The beauty of Mother Earth

We can find within each other

I Am II

I am the rain

I am the tree

I am the flower

I am the bee

As I look within myself

I finally see

There is no difference between

Mother Nature and Me

Seasons

I have experienced many deaths

Layers falling away like autumn leaves

Or violently ripped away

But every death revealed life

Every death led me home

Bare

And just like that, I want to start again. The things I own and wear and touch mean nothing. There is deeper meaning within me. Yet, I recognize so much of myself in these things.

If I threw them all away

Danced naked in the emptiness

Laughed at all the silly things

Draped in only my skin

Then, can I easily reach my soul?

Reflections

I look out into the world, and I feel its stillness. I sit and watch the trees grow silently. The clouds float by at ease, without a destination. I acknowledge this peace I feel within myself. Mother Earth is a reflection of what is inside of us all.

The way we choose to look at the world is the way the world will look back.

Children of the Sun

It's okay to want to laugh

And sing and dance and play

We are all children of the sun

And together

We will return to the moon

And stars one day

Sanctuary

How incredible is it

To feel safe in my own skin

To feel at home

We rise and we fall

Our darkness

Lifted by the wind

Kissed by the rain

Guided by the light

We learn to begin again

Scorpio

I am just as powerful as

The cosmos above me

Just as wise as

The roots entangled beneath me

Gentler than the setting sun

And as cunning as the moon

Fuck Your System

I am doing things so differently

Than everyone around me

I am not working for a degree

A pat on the back from someone who doesn't even know me

Let me speak

Let me dream

I will be loud with my words

I will always follow my dreams

Even if it's risky

I will not risk keeping my voice bottled up

My words hold too much truth

The power to connect me to you

The power to raise this planets frequency

So yes

I do things differently

I had to jump in order to be free

Shine Bright

You never know who is in the dark

Praying for a glimpse of the light

Dreams

Every day is my canvas

Where my imagination flows

A blank page for my dreams to wander

As far as I'll let them go

And just like a planted seed

Patiently over time

They will bloom into sweet flowers

Right before my eyes

Affirm:

I Am Worthy In My Being

Boundaries

Please do not tell me

Who or what to be

I am not your creation

You are not allowed

To cloud

My authenticity

128

A Poem of What a Woman Can Be

A woman can be

Powerfully calm

A peaceful warrior

A rose who keeps her thorns

She is the ocean and its waves

She is sexual and sensual

She is not black or white

She is every color

And most importantly

She is

Whatever she wants to be

Goddess

Her liquid gold skin is magic

Her energy will meet you in your dreams

Her body is a temple

A guardian and a best friend

Her hips hold the wisdom of her ancestors

Breasts mimicking mountains

Stretch marks like the rings within a tree

Her Loud Soul will set you free

To All of My Sisters

Your hands have done so much already

Crafted your entire life

You are so worthy

Of all that you dream

Our hearts crack others open

Our voices heal and mend

Our pussies are portals

To the oneness within

Keep shining

Keep gleaming

You are so powerful my friend

Simply Worthy

Your worth is not a competition

Your worth is not another's "I love you"

Your worth is not your past or future

You are simply worthy because you woke up today

You are simply worthy

You May Not Feel Me Now

I'm too afraid to say goodbye

So I pray for a new day

A new me and a new you

You may not feel me now

But one day I'll meet you in the sky

Where we can fly and laugh at how simple things
could have been

And how simple things are now

My wish is to feel the peace I send to future me

I open my eyes and my heart to see

How easy it is to truly be free

3:33

Safety will never fulfill our Loud Souls

The End For Now

Mya G. Wolf has been inspired by the world around her ever since a young age. She is moved by the beauty of mother nature and is drawn to the complexity of being human. Mya uses poetry to turn her interests into a form of art. Her words are channeled directly from her heart in hopes to empower and uplift her readers.

Although this is Mya's first collection of poetry, it certainly won't be her last. She will always be inspired to share her words with the world.

Printed in Great Britain
by Amazon